Cardiff Soul

Cardiff Soul

an underground guide to the city

Colin Palfrey

y **L**_olfa_

To my parents, who enabled me to be born in the capital city
of the most talented nation in the world.

Thanks to my son, Gareth, for carrying out
some of the interviews.

First impression: 2006
© Colin Palfrey and Y Lolfa Cyf., 2006

Cover design: Y Lolfa

ISBN: 0 86243 909 4
ISBN: 9 780862 439095

Printed on acid-free and partly recycled paper
and published and bound in Wales by
Y Lolfa Cyf., Talybont, Ceredigion SY24 5AP
e-mail ylolfa@ylolfa.com
website www.ylolfa.com
tel 01970 832 304
fax 832 782

Contents

Cardiff Soul 1

Where is Cardiff's soul? What makes the city tick? Does it have a unique character, a real centre, a heart?

Is Piccadilly Circus the soul of London or the Eiffel Tower the heart of Paris? There are buildings and monuments that spring to mind when we try to imagine a particular place.

It's probably the familiar that makes you want to stay in a city that you like or even love. But the familiar can be ugly and repellent. It's the root of 'familiar' I'm talking about here – the family. Yes – families can be dysfunctional, but if you're dysfunctional yourself, that's where you'd feel at home. So for all its unattractiveness, its blemishes, its shortcomings – or even because of them – a city can make you never want to leave; the familiar works for you.

But before we become too solemn, let's make it clear that this book is not about the history of Cardiff. That's been covered in many volumes replete with photographs of men and boys in cloth caps and boots (and, of course, other clothes), horse-drawn carriages, bewhiskered shopkeepers standing with pinafores on display outside their shop-fronts and women without the hint of a limb showing. Perhaps all those old photos were taken in winter.

This book is about Cardiff today – in 2006 – when young women display midriffs all year round and on Friday and Saturday nights, even when temperatures are sub-zero, cavort in bits of material just about enough to make a man's handkerchief.

Cardiff is not chic or elegant. It's down to earth.

The city is large enough to offer a wealth of experiences, musical, theatrical, sporting, but small enough to suppress any attempts at pretentiousness. Charlotte Church should be its patron saint. St Charlotte sounds right and, what's more, since we're soul-searching here, her surname has a certain ring about it. Dame Shirley – yes; but never St Shirley. It just doesn't have that ecclesiastical tone.

Today, in the new millennium, Cardiff stands proud in the knowledge that it probably has the highest number of traffic calmers (bumps in the road) per head of population, or even bottom of population, in the whole of Europe. The Splott and Tremorfa areas are particularly well-blessed. If any more are built into the streets here, they will soon all join up and will form the first elevated roadway in Wales (apart from the Gabalfa flyover and the various bridges, which don't count).

In the first decade of the millennium, Cardiff can also boast perhaps the most macabre building in the world – a vast monument to the living dead. This is called the Welsh Assembly or *senedd*. In a palatial modern edifice, strange rituals are performed almost daily by men and women who live in a twilight world between devolution and self-government. There is a person of high office called First Minister who speaks in strange tongues none of which, to the ordinary person, makes any sense. They are lost – poor souls – in limbo.

This, then, is the very last place to find the soul of Cardiff.

Whether Cardiff has a soul we can leave aside for the moment. We can look at what it has got, what it hasn't, and talk to some of the people who live here. As we move along charting various aspects of city life, perhaps – at the end of this little journey – we might have found *Cardiff's Soul*. That could be a prize worth waiting for.

Past and present

Of course, you could argue that the soul of a city can change, but that seems to be a contradiction. Can souls change? In theological terms no, but the soul of a city – in the sense of its defining character – can change over time.

Visually, two buildings dominate Cardiff: the castle and the Millennium Stadium. But, as we shall argue later, the visual appeal does not necessarily lie in such grandiose structures, but rather in the more modest domestic buildings, or in the architectural detailed embellishments above shops along St Mary Street and Queen Street. There are some impressive churches, chapels, and arcades of shops. These sheltered shopping walkways are a feature of the city. They contain some of the more original outlets for specialist goods and provide a healthy antidote to the large chain stores that dominate most urban landscapes.

It's a cliché to state that the past shapes and informs the present but the former docks area of Cardiff played host to a multitude of different people from distant parts and, over many years, this gentle influx has not led to social disruption or enmity. But this was not always the case. In the 19th century there were sporadic riots between some inhabitants and Irish immigrants seeking work. This evoked memories among some historians of the skirmishes around the castle in the third century AD when Irish invaders lay siege. Today, there are few more loyal Cardiffians than those of Irish origin.

Cardiff has a proud recent record of racial and ethnic tolerance, if not complete integration or equity in terms of income and job opportunities. Because we, the Welsh, have been underdogs politically and economically for so many decades, perhaps we can feel something of a bond between ourselves and others from ethnic minorities. Welsh people are, in the context of the UK, an ethnic minority living in a land annexed by England. And yet, despite the many attempts by invading aggressors to put down the unruly inhabitants of this small nation, we have cussedly refused to let the Welsh language be extinguished and we remain probably more at ease with Celtic 'tribes' at a distance from us than with our immediate neighbours.

And since rugby is as close as you can get nowadays to open warfare, while we shrug our collective shoulders if we lose to Scotland or Ireland, we almost have a week of mourning if we lose to England. However, there are other, more parochial divisions. Many people from the south Wales valleys will tell you that they still feel insecure when they think of Cardiff; some Cardiffians, meanwhile, apparently regard anywhere north of Cardiff as the end of civilisation.

But Cardiff *is* the capital city of Wales – not a universally popular choice, according to many people in Wales who regard it as less Welsh than some more western or northern towns. But then what is being Welsh? It can't be the capacity to speak Welsh; it goes much deeper than that. ID cards and passports tell officials who you are but don't have anything to say about how you feel. Identity is personal, so if you see photographs of certain landmarks in Cardiff you can associate them with that city. But if you photographed a thousand people who live in Cardiff and who love the city they could be from any Welsh or British city.

Think of some currently well-known Cardiff personalities: the singer and songwriter Frank Hennessy; multi-medallist and athlete Tanni Grey-Thompson; the 'Cardiff boy' journalist Dan O'Neill; the athlete Colin Jackson and former Welsh rugby international Nigel Walker; White? Irish? Black? No – all of them Welsh Cardiffians.

The 'old' Cardiff is what used to be called working-class – Splott, Grangetown, Adamsdown, Roath. The later Cardiff was mainly middle class: Cyncoed, Llandaff, Llanishen and the even newer bits of Cardiff were – if you were a pupil at one of the better grammar schools in Cardiff – considered to be hillbilly country – Pentyrch, Tongwynlais, Creigiau. Now we're all Cardiffians, at least in the eyes of Cardiff County Council who collect the council tax from Tremorfa to Gwaelod-y-garth.

So – past-present; old and new. Cardiff consists of opposites. It is both Beauty and the Beast.

Beauty and the Beast

If the Germans had bombed the civic centre, what would Cardiff have had left in the way of grand or even aesthetically-pleasing buildings? Answers please on the back of a second class stamp! Even the castle, the vestige of vindictive imperialism, has none of the splendour of Harlech or Caernarfon castles. Its surrounding walls are modern, the precursor of the hideous stone cladding defacing modest terraces up and down Wales.

But the pompous symmetry of the area featuring the National Museum, the City Hall and former county hall, the law courts and the Temple of Peace has been disfigured by the crass utilitarianism of extensions to the university buildings. There is no visual beauty in Cardiff streets. The rigid and uniform terraces of Edwardian Cathedral Road and Ninian Road have a certain aura of affluent respectability but add little grace to the urban landscape.

The **Wales Millennium Centre** is the much-vaunted new arts centre that stages musicals, ballet, opera and other artistic performances. On the ground floor you can listen to free performances by unknown musicians and singers – classical, jazz and some more off-beat music. The Urdd, literature agency Academi and the dance group Diversions are based here. The centre's architectural novelty is in its visual resemblance to an armadillo, and the English and Welsh poetical snippets hewn out of its frontage. The letters of the poetic lines are see-through. The poetic titbits are for me pretty meaningless in either language: the English proclaims:

'In these stones horizons sing' – too deep for me, while the Welsh is: 'Creating truth like glass from inspiration's furnace'. What version of the truth you'd get from an arts centre is to my mind debatable and the two esses in 'horizons sing' do not strike me as being melodious.

The shape of the edifice is merely a more stolid version of the nautical syndrome that characterises several buildings in the Bay. Enter the building from the main access point and you will find yourself in a huge airport booking-in palace – apologies for the unintended play on words.

Inside the theatre – or auditorium if Latin is preferred – you will be surrounded by the work of a demented artex fiend. The walls are covered in muddy orange representations of rocky outcrops. The effect is of watching 21st-century performers in a prehistoric cave. The whole exterior is a mishmash of slate, wood and rock with a reception area so dark in its décor that it brings to mind the old adage of 'suffering for one's art'. The building's creators seem to be saying: if you come to see or listen to high-grade performances, be prepared to feel uncomfortable. An evening out here – apart from at the tapas bar – is a form of artistic penance.

Far more pleasant on the eye than this huge monument are the sumptuous porch tiles in the modest houses in Moorland Road in Splott and in other less ostentatious strings of houses in Grangetown. The economic boom in the early years of the twentieth century and the slum-clearance epidemic of the 1950s erased swathes of green and the *jolie-laide* rows of old terraces. But thankfully delicate flourishes are still evident on many Cardiff houses, and show up the blank uncaring architecture that blights many housing estates. Compare, for example, the inventiveness of the row of linked buildings in Moira Terrace in Adamsdown and their protruding green-painted buttress windows with later attempts at housing in or near the centre of the city. Now there are no new terraced houses being built. Their counterparts are the vertically-terraced blocks littering the access roads to the Bay.

The saving grace of Cardiff is that you can escape its soulless buildings because of the multiplicity of parkland – from the vastness of the land north of the castle to Roath Park in the east of the city and the numerous mini-oases shared by nearly every old suburb. Let's talk about the new, vibrant ex-Docks area later. Enough to say at this point that the new residential buildings in 'The Bay' look across or down on the most economically-deprived area in Wales; part of the old Docks. The result is that some of the most affluent residents of Cardiff are within a short walk away from the most economically deprived. This is the kind of contrast that turns pessimists to indulge in nostalgia and optimists to relish the challenge of the future. We'll slip in between.

Cardiff now

Progress is a deceptive concept: moving forward, keeping ahead of the game, thrusting, invigorating, the WOW factor. Only old codgers live in the past. Look at what Cardiff has now – the Cardiff International Arena, St David's Hall, the Millennium Stadium, shopping malls, chic bars, an ice rink (soon to re-locate down the Bay). So it's lost all its old cinemas, but there are new multiplex cinemas dotted all around. The racecourse, speedway track and roller-skating venues have gone, but nobody's built over the bowling greens yet, and though chapels are being converted into cheapjack retail outlets, Cardiff still has an impressive thriving secular

Cardiff International Arena

chapel – a bingo hall. Heaven forbid that it should ever be used in the future as a chapel.

Now maybe that's where we could look for the soul of Cardiff. No – most large towns have bingo halls. But it is impressive: the preacher calling the numbers; the hushed congregation, eyes glued to the text and then a shout of exultation – the hallelujah of – the evangelical cry of 'HOUSE!' Rapture for some; and for the disappointed, always the prospect of fulfilment next week.

> *"And you know – there was a dance every Saturday night in the City Hall with a live band and bright lights."*
>
> *"Never, Granddad. Did you go?"*
>
> *"Oh yes."*
>
> *"And you danced?"*
>
> *"Oh no. We just talked – at least we could hear ourselves talk in those days. There were a few clubs where you could drink after hours but it was all civilised. Not like now – with binge-drinking and fighting in the streets."*
>
> *"Did you ever get drunk, Granddad?"*
>
> *"Well, occasionally, but we were students so binge-drinking then was called having a good time and any fighting was just high spirits."*
>
> *"Oh."*

Cardiff must be a real city because it's got massage parlours, and you can hire escorts for the night. That's pretty chic and sophisticated. In the old days there were prostitutes up and down Westgate Street and down the docks. So I'm told. And isn't there at least one lap-dancing club where nobody from Cardiff goes, in case they're seen by one of the neighbours or someone from work.

> *"Oh hello Dave. I thought this was just an ordinary bar.*
> *But I suppose I'd better stay now. How's your good lady*
> *wife...?"*

And are you telling me there's a couple of no-smoking pubs in
Cardiff? That's amazing. I remember a pub crawl in Canton,
a mile or less from the city centre, and in one of the pubs was
a no-smoking area where everyone was smoking. The blokes,
pot-bellied and fortyish, were in their weekend best – neatly
ironed white vests that showed up their flabby-armed tattoos.
I wasn't too inclined to demand they stopped smoking in there
as they puffed aggressively under the No Smoking sign. But
more of this later.

Vests are in vogue – at least among certain patrons of
supermarkets. I wonder if men wander down the aisles of
Asda in vests, say in Edinburgh or Rome. Has Asda reached
Rome? If not, perhaps this fashion feature could mark
Cardiff out as unique. Are vests the soul of Cardiff? It must
have something to do with shopping in supermarkets. I
haven't yet spotted a concertgoer in St David's Hall decked
out in a shining white string vest during a Mozart concert,
or at the New Theatre, or at the artistic railway station
known as the Millennium Arts Centre. Oh yes – I'll come
back to that again.

My hypothesis is that pushing a heavy trolley full of
lager, crisps and sausages is a strenuous physical challenge
especially for men whose stomachs prevent their arms from
grasping the trolley handlebars very firmly. Remaining cool
in those circumstances demands appropriate clothing. The
wimpish middle class never fill their trolleys with enough
goodies to necessitate stripping down to their underwear.
I've seen their trolley contents, especially in Sainsbury's –

all yoghurt and bran flakes. A three-year-old could push that around.

And while we're in Sainsbury's, we can mention their policy of taking on employees who are over 50. That's very enlightened. But I heard on a radio programme that one listener's granddad, who was 78 and working in Sainsbury's, had an appraisal with a view to a pay rise. Sadly, he was not awarded the pay rise because his appraisal report stated that he "showed no ambition within the organisation." You can imagine the line manager saying: "Tell me, Arnold, where do you want to be in 10 years' time?" and Arnold replies: "Hopefully, still on the planet". It just shows that being honest gets you nowhere.

St David's Hall

Food

Of course, you can have a complete day out in some of these supermarkets. Some are open 24 hours, like Tesco Extra near Gabalfa. Probably others do as well. A female friend who by choice has no children reckoned she could offer a brilliant service to some of the big supermarkets in Cardiff – or anywhere else for that matter. She could control screaming kids. As they screamed from aisle to aisle she would offer, on a sliding scale of fees, a quick slap right up to a sustained thrashing. But in this world of political and every other type of social correctness, she probably wouldn't earn a lot. So she has to make do with her partner.

Don't bother eating in any of the supermarkets. They have about as much ambience as a church hall and the range and quality of food resembles a bad day out in Butlins.

So, if you want a memorable meal in Cardiff where do you go? I asked three people I was with recently which restaurant they would recommend to someone for a really outstanding meal. They suddenly went quiet. There are plenty of places you can go to in Cardiff to have a memorably bad meal or an unforgettably mediocre meal. But is there somewhere you can eat which transports you to another level of gastronomic experience? OK – that's a bit extreme. What about settling for outstanding value for money. No, we need to rephrase that, because until the prices recently went up, the Hayes Island Snack bar produced giant hot dogs that were really good value, but hardly *haute cuisine* – hot cuisine, but not *haute*.

The restaurant that keeps being mentioned as a cut above the rest is Le Gallois in Romilly Road. Before this book is finished I hope to win enough money on the lottery to try it and report back.

What you *can* say about the eating places in Cardiff is that there is plenty of choice as far as ethnicity is concerned. *Buzz* magazine does a really good round-up of cafes and restaurants so don't listen to me. Most of my taste buds died years ago – and is that the reason why I believe there is no first-rate Indian/Bangladeshi restaurant in Cardiff? I compare them with the ones of yesteryear: the Star of India in Bridge Street and the Bay Bombay in Bute Street – which was transformed into a 'modern' Indian restaurant very recently. What! No flock wallpaper? But over the road, occupying a small space in a kebab take-away, is what remains of the Bay Bombay – now just a take-away itself.

Jinuk in Canton is good but I had to ask them to turn off the nauseating muzak and put on a tape of authentic curry music. The food improved with the mood. The trouble is that so-called Indian food is now so popular much of it on offer has reduced itself to the lowest common denominator. What are the three top dishes in Cardiff? Balti, chicken tikka massala and anything with chicken 'half and half'. Let's do a Gordon Ramsay on these Welsh delicacies.

Balti, which originated in the exotic setting of Birmingham, is the dish (or, literally, the 'bucket') the food is cooked in: a kind of Indian wok. The result is an endless catalogue of bland tomato-stricken dishes that are about as exciting as a wet afternoon in Barry. Chicken tikka massala is non-threatening; a mix of the sweet and the gooey. Try pasanda. That's really sweet. And half and half – a mix of rice and chips – a delicacy apparently unknown outside Wales. Don't let me get into unsavoury comments about the food of the Cardiff low-life. This is the food of vests.

The one gold standard of Indian cooking is rogan gosht which should be the most subtle blend of spices garnished with tomatoes. Trust me – there isn't one restaurant or take away in the whole of Cardiff that passes this litmus test of exotic cooking. Most Indian/Bangladeshi food served in Cardiff looks and tastes as if the chef has shares in an off-shore oil rig. In one year, eating an Indian meal once a fortnight, you would have consumed more oil than it would take to run a Maserati over a lifetime. So, if there is anyone out there who can recommend an Indian restaurant that is above the common multitude of mediocrity, I'll pay for a meal for them and a partner plus drinks; if it's run of the mill I'll just pay for my own meal.

First it was Indian and Chinese; now the modern craze is for tapas – a selection of Spanish dishes served as a variety of titbits. The one not to go to in Cardiff is the one down the bay that advertises tapas but is usually not able to serve you any food unless you arrive there between the hours of 1.30 and 1.35. But the one in the Brewery Quarter by Caroline Street is very good if you don't mind eating smoked dishes – that is dishes served with other patrons' cigarette smoke – but not for much longer as the no-smoking legislation is brought in. But a revelation in the new Cardiff airport – aka the Millennium Centre (I'll definitely come back to that) – is the unostentatious little bar known as **ONE**. The staff represent most of Europe and, not surprisingly, seem to care about customers. The atmosphere is gentle and continental. Seats are hard (more plush upstairs) but not as hard as those in Chapter (I'll also come back to that). As I write, another tapas place – Pica Pica – has opened in Westgate Street.

But are these immigrant culinary offerings the soul of Cardiff? Hardly. There must be some more homely eating places. What about the indigenous greasy spoons? (Why 'spoons'? Most people don't use spoons in caffs. Some don't even use forks.)

Further west you could be offered a full cholesterol breakfast with laver bread and cockles. Only our eccentric cousins west of Bridgend could have come up with seaweed and salty tooth-fillings as potential fodder for the Welsh palate. Why not ragwort or sea-kale or sand?

So where shall we go to savour the truckers' delight? Roath and Splott areas are good places to start. There are two on Clifton Street but the Ideal Café on Broadway is no more - it was good but not ideal. But also try the **Carlisle Bakery** near the STAR Leisure Centre. It's clean and serves the full cholesterol breakfast all day. A well-known and well-patronised caff is the **Black and White** on Penarth Road not far from the Cardiff City ground and **Rosario's** on Caroline Street – dark and brooding. Clean, green and sporting gingham curtains, **Gorge with George** on Bute Street is another caff but falls short of the real thing because it does not include any fried bread in the cooked breakfast or even real tomatoes. So this does not qualify as a bona fide greasy spoon; only a smeary spoon. Even in the exalted region of Cyncoed there is a bakery-cum-caff – opposite the Discovery pub – which offers a fried breakfast.

What's great about greasy spoons is the quality control. You get what you expect; none of the anxious anticipation about whether the truffles are really mushrooms in disguise or whether the Chablis might be from the wrong end of the vineyard. Bacon is bacon and a fried egg is never going to be from the wrong end of the hen. Mind you, if you could ever breed hens that actually laid eggs already fried you'd make a fortune.

What Cardiff doesn't have is a really first-class coffee house. There are plenty around in the centre and the suburbs, but there's not much class about them. The coffee houses of old in the eighteenth century would have had an atmosphere, so we read, of elegance and artistic conversation. What do we have in Cardiff? Please don't mention Starbucks. What beacons of good taste America has given us? McDonald's, the Hard Rock Café and Starbucks. Anyone prepared to pay more than double the going rate for a coffee and sit in an atmosphere redolent of a pre-war railway station waiting room is welcome to patronise Starbucks or any of the other graceless coffee places dotted around.

One or two such as the **Café Aroma** on Crwys Road are nearly there: relaxed, welcoming, unpretentiously priced. There is also the Coffee House or **Tŷ Coffi** on Wellfield Road that offers a reasonable variety of coffee and snacks. Across the road was FT5K, which stands for 'Feed the 5 Thousand'. Why? That an establishment that at 9.15 in the morning could not produce a bacon baguette because they had no baguettes shows the depths to which some food outlets can descend. Yet it started out promisingly in one of the shopping complexes in the city centre. That's closed, but there is still one left down the Bay where restaurants come and go like ships in the night. Perhaps in the Pontcanna area the **Café Brava** is worth a visit – home to luvvies and dog walkers: try ordering 'eggs benedict' in Splott!

I seem to be talking a lot about food. *Pour moi* (as they say in Tremorfa), food and drink excite me, or more specifically, the prospect and anticipation of high-quality food and drink make life almost worth living.

So we continue. I must return to the **Devonia** fish and chip shop at the Gabalfa end of Whitchurch Road. It's one of the few takeaways that was there when I was a lad. Is it as good as it looks? Before this work is completed I'm going to buy a feast of British stodge and let you know the verdict. I might even break my resolution not to eat dead cow and order a Clark's pie to go with the chips. As a good friend and colleague of mine declares: you can't be indifferent to a Clark's pie. This Cardiff family has been making these unique offerings for seventy-five years. Don't ever, ever, ever put a Clark's pie in a microwave. Its magic lies in the pastry which dissolves into a glutinous mess in the microwave. There ought to be a by-law in Cardiff that would make that an offence punishable by a compulsory meal at a particular over-hyped fish and chip restaurant in Cardiff Bay. The thought is too painful to dwell on.

According to that arch-exponent of the Cardiff accent and vernacular, Frank Hennessy, the Millennium Stadium was modelled on the Clark's pie. An aerial view of it with the roof closed, he reckons, looks just like a Clarkie's with a cocktail stick at each round corner.

So on the theme of fish and chips we move across the city to Chip Alley – **Caroline Street**. This haven of life-affirming downmarket fast-food is threatened on one of its sides by the encroachment of quasi-sophisticated eating places. There is something noble about a street full of seemingly squalid eating places and something squalid about 'cool' bars and restaurants. That's why the docks held much more fascination for me than the Bay will ever generate. Just look what's happened visually. Watch the film Tiger Bay and you'll see dark little alleyways, threatening, exciting, raw and dishevelled. Now the skyline of the Bay is stunningly naïve in its attempt to pretend that they are actually ships or nautical appendages. So dolphins leap on top of buildings and even the Millennium Stadium, inland but on the banks of the RiverTaff, has a web of yardarms but without the sails.

Probably the greatest missed opportunity in the whole of Cardiff is the caff in Roath Park although there are now strong rumours that this opportunity is about to be grasped. This semi-rotunda plus patio area is situated on the side of the lake but closes when the rest of the gated parts of the park close. Why is there a time limit? What are our esteemed city fathers and mothers, grandfathers and grandmothers and any other varieties of kinship actually protecting? The only things of value are the swans, geese and ducks and if you want one of these for the occasional barbecue there is access all around the lake. You could of course end up in prison if you nabbed a swan so better make do with a pheasant – a much more impressive creature that should have a preservation order on it. Imagine a first-class cuisine served up in a restaurant overlooking the lake. At the moment the nearest you'll get to an aquatic culinary experience is taking a packed lunch with you on one of the rowing boats. 'Come in Number 5 – you've had your pudding!'

Hotels

Cardiff must have the greatest number of hotels per square metre in the UK. These range from the 5-star Hilton and St David's to the more modest The Big Sleep and Ibis. The original hotels of a more gracious era still survive: the Angel, and the former Park Hotel, now the Thistle, still proclaim an earlier vintage of elegance. Nowadays the big side-attraction in hotels is the health suite. The very recently established **Macdonald Holland House** is one of the leading hotels offering hedonistic indulgence to people (i e women) who are prepared to pay the price of a small car to have hot stones placed on their bare flesh and to have mud plastered over their faces. Most building sites could offer this type of treatment at a fraction of the cost!

Several of the grand turn-of-the-century houses along Cathedral Road have become small hotels or rather grand B&Bs and the more modest establishments on Newport Road have been transformed into shabby-genteel hotels. Somewhat more down-market are the massage parlours which, like the term 'escort', cloak their real activities behind a coy euphemism. Some places offering massages are presumably just that, but beware of signing in for treatment for a sporting injury or slipped disc at what could turn out to be a brothel, although perhaps the treatment could be classified as alternative therapy. Similarly, avoid talking animatedly about your unhappy marriage and sensual fantasies to what might be a somewhat alarmed physiotherapist.

One out-of-town hotel (but still in Cardiff) that is

worth a visit is the **Village** at the top end of Whitchurch on the Coryton roundabout. It has a leisure club with the best swimming pool of any other hotel or council leisure centre in Cardiff; a coffee house, decent restaurant and a pub that sells real ale. It's clean, comfortable and convenient with ample parking space. The idea is to exercise enough to work up a thirst and an appetite; then put the calories back on in the bar and restaurant. What's more, here you can get a real massage and an unreal tan, but with all the joss sticks burning in the Beauty Suite, you could come out smelling as if you've just been visiting/working in a downtown Hong Kong palace of pleasure.

But hotels are usually soulless places – the habitat of business people and non-locals. We need to seek out the soul of Cardiff in more down-to-earth resorts such as pubs. The word 'pub' seems far less warm and welcoming than an 'inn'. The **Holiday Inn** at one end of Westgate Street is not an inn or a pub. It's a middling hotel; functional and ordinary. So what about the pubs of Cardiff?

Pubs and bars

Where would you go to find local characters? One place is the 'local'. But in a city, by definition, there are no 'locals' – perhaps in the suburbs but probably not in the city centre. So we are not going to find the soul of Cardiff in a pub. Perhaps we should look instead for pubs with 'character'. There used to be quite a few. Take away the **Golden Cross** with its officially-preserved tiles and the **Vulcan**, threatened with demolition, and there's not much left.

An example of the desecration of a pub with character is the George, at the confluence of Richmond Road, City Road, and Albany Road. This pub had very impressive wood panelling, probably unique in Cardiff, but the brewery – genuflecting on the altar of youth – took it all away and the pub is now a featureless reproduction of every other tatty drinking hole in and around the city. I can no longer enter the Old Arcade in Church Street either. Some vandal took out the beautiful etched windows to open up the front bar so that patrons can sit outside – on how many days a year in our climate? There are plenty of people living in Cardiff or who own property in Cardiff who have no soul.

Of course, we try not to use the word 'pub' any more. That's dated. We now have 'bars'. These all have bouncers on the door to make sure that nobody over the age of 25 can get in. You don't find bouncers at the portals of pubs. There is no more depressing a sight than watching hordes of pubescent youngsters queuing to gain access in the early hours to a bar in order to void the contents of their stomachs three hours later. The problem is they drink gassy stuff and mix it with other even more gassy stuff. As the males continue in this career of self-abuse the stomach becomes distended to such an extent that it defies the law of gravity and belts must give way to braces. Lager – 'light' ale – is for drinking in hot countries, not in rainy Wales. We need a drink that is more in keeping with our environment; something tepid and a bit old-fashioned. But...

Whatever happened to beer? Unless you are a devotee of Brains offerings, the whole city is a desert. The Glasshouse (now re-named Copa) at the side of Howells store used to provide a range of real ales. Not any more. It's now changed its name and has wiped out nearly every real ale it ever had except for Guinness – but that's not ale; it's stout.

One pub that had character was the former Cambrian on the corner of Caroline Street. It's now – would you believe – an Irish bar. The Cambrian was the only pub in the city centre where, on rugby international days, you wouldn't have to scrum your head down and force your way in. This was because of the ambience: no tables, no chairs and three inches or the metric equivalent of slops on the floor. Falling down in this, as many did, was to risk a very squelchy death by drowning.

There is one exception to the trend towards lager-laden bars in Cardiff and that is the **Weatherspoon** chain of pubs. Can you imagine a boardroom discussion along these lines:

"What about opening up a few pubs in the middle of cities in Britain that have a strict no-smoking area, no music in the background or foreground and where there is a good range of real ales served at two thirds the price of most beers."

Stunned silence followed by studied guffaws.

"Keep taking the tablets. You'll be OK tomorrow – ha, ha."

But it's worked and, would you believe, even people under the age of 25 seem to enjoy being in these pubs. They also serve decent food and you can go there for breakfast. Somehow, the owner of the Weatherspoon chain latched onto the idea of offering good service at value-for-money prices. What an incredibly innovative idea in the context of the British food and drink trade.

We'll add another pub that manages to combine a relatively up-market image with the feel of a real ale pub: the **Pen and Wig** behind Park Place. This has managed to do what the Eli Jenkins down the Bay has failed to do – that is, recreate the identity of a traditional pub even though it's a new building. The Eli Jenkins is a dingy, instantly down-at-heel establishment with a poor range of beers. But – to its credit – at least it's a pub, not a bar.

Nowadays there is a move towards whole pubs becoming fag-free. Two recent additions to the very short list are **The Cottage** in St Mary Street – a real pub, and 33 Windsor Place, known plainly as **33.** This bar-cum-eating-place is minimalist, clean, serves good food, and offers efficient and friendly service. The down side? It's an exclusively Brains place, but the house wine is excellent. Even **Chapter**, the arch-arty venue has banned smoking indoors and has erected a canopy outdoors for the weedos.

Chapter? You mean the spot where they used to frisk you for spliffs on the door and not let you in unless you had some on you? (Don't sue. It's a joke.) Yes – Chapter. What next? Well, one futuristic vision is for smokers to be banned from entering St David's Hall with or without cigarettes. I have a picture in my mind that one day the conductor of the symphony orchestra will turn to the audience after a bit of tuning up, and conduct the coughing. Wouldn't it be satisfying to listen to Mozart without an accompanying chorus of wheezing and spluttering? Forget about banning smoking in public places. Smokers should be banned from buying tickets to classical concerts.

But back to pubs. Take a look at the most recent *Good Pub Guide to Britain* and you will not find a single Cardiff pub included. "Well," rants the landlord of a city centre pub in the local paper, "the people who come around checking us out are just the green welly brigade – all real-ale-and-no-juke-boxes. We can't please them, but we've got our customers so we must be OK." He has a point. His pub is no worse than most in the city centre. It's drab, noisy and smoke-infested, but being close to the Millennium Stadium it has little need to start primping itself up for a more discriminating clientele – such as grumpy old men who smoke pipes and wear sandals underneath their green wellies – or are those the grumpy old women? However, this same pub – along with many others in the city centre, was given a rating of nought out of ten on the Cardiff website and that's probably a bit generous.

Perhaps we're looking for the soul of Cardiff in the wrong place. Since most of us have no idea where the human soul resides or even if we have one, let's think laterally and look outwards to the city suburbs – especially for food and drink and, of course, for real people. Nobody actually lives in the city centre except for the enigmatic denizens of the newly-raised inner city flats – sorry – apartments. I have been inside one or two and they are seductively appointed with all mod cons and a newness that speaks of a clientele with over-used credit cards.

Those which were once the Automobile Association headquarters near Queen Street station look as if a prison has been turned inside out: stark, grim balconies almost invite the residents to escape by jumping into the street below. Those in and around the Bay are strictly for sheep in human form: the kind of people who are mesmerised by newness and follow the trail to the estate agent as if abducted by aliens. They represent the R (for recently-rich)-Soul of Cardiff.

Canton – not, as you and I might think, an echo of Cardiff's zenith as a magnet for shipping and oriental incomers – a distant replicated region of China – but, much more prosaically, a settlement on a brook known as Canna, as in Pontcanna. Similarly, Cathays – the university quarter – is not etymologically rooted in the old name for China but apparently stems from an old English word for hedge joined to an old Welsh word for battle. How boring.

Canton could be the soul of Cardiff. It has a lot in its favour: multi-cultural eating places, real pubs, an arts centre, decent shops, almost a village atmosphere, and a mix of socio-economic groups – a euphemism for different classes. It has **Chapter** (see above) – a former school transformed into a sort of multiplex arts emporium. It has a cinema, a theatre, rooms to hire for dance sessions, smaller spaces for intimate gigs. It hosts film seasons, avant garde art exhibitions – one of the latest being a woman 'artist' who drank 48 bottles of beer and then walked on a gymnast's beam in her high heels. Could this develop into a new Olympic event? Chapter has the largest range of lagers in town, that is, almost respectable lagers from abroad and in bottles, with four ales available.

The food there was merely passable but now, with

a recently-appointed chef, it is much improved, but the seating is still monastic and unyielding. This is a pity because you shouldn't have to suffer for art; that notion went out of the window post-nineteenth century. A little comfort isn't a short cut to decadence and, in any case, what's a little decadence between artistic friends?

Some suburban pubs are worth a look-in. The **Discovery** in Cyncoed has a good range of beers, but at a somewhat inflated price since you drink them in one of the most affluent quarters in Cardiff. Inside the **Albany** in Donald Street, Roath it still seems more like someone's large living room than a pub – an original public house. In Whitchurch there are two pubs within the space of a few strides – the **Plough** and **Royal Oak.** These are unspoiled, old-fashioned pubs and there are others, but you will have to go to other suburbs of the city.

But enough of these plebeian haunts. Where do you go if you want to catch a glimpse of a 'personality' out on the town? The hot tip is to make for **Backpackers** in the Riverside district, the **Soda Bar** in St Mary Street or the **Cameo Club** in Pontcanna. Singers, actors and media people can be seen in such places and a favourite haunt of rugby players is **Life**, also in St Mary Street. But if you would prefer to join a club that would probably not allow any of these often wayward people to become members, have a look at the new **Park House Club** in Park Place. Occupying a neo-Gothic Grade 1 listed building designed by William Burges (the fevered brain behind the interior tatty opulence of the Cardiff Castle and the fantasy called Castell Coch to the north of Cardiff), the club is an oasis of gentility in an increasingly boorish urban desert.

Some pubs, such as the **Plough** in Whitchurch and the **Butchers Arms** in Rhiwbina, still have their bowling alleys and there is a league or two in Cardiff devoted to this traditional pastime. Shove-ha'penny and cribbage have gone, but the bowls alley and darts carry on. But as in many aspects of city life, new – often American – pastimes, have taken over. So now we have ten-pin bowling centres in Cardiff, on Newport Road and in the **Red Dragon Centre,** the multi-activity facility in the Bay, which also houses a cinema, restaurants, night-life and a casino.

With ten-pin bowling you can choose different-weighted bowls so women can compete on a level playing field or even-more-level bowling alley against men. The main thing apparently is to choose a bowl that can accommodate your fingers comfortably, otherwise you run the risk, if your fingers are too large for the holes in the bowl, of ending up hurling yourself still attached to the bowl and knocking down the pins with your head which, I assume, would constitute a foul.

Let's go outside for a while, away from the pubs, bars, restaurants and hotels. Breathe the questionable air into our lungs and search for the soul of Cardiff in the cramped outdoors – but dipping indoors occasionally to meet and interact with real people.

Markets and street traders

Markets are magic. They transform buying into something more personal. In most cases the person behind the stall is the owner. The transaction is direct and immediate. In the centre of Cardiff there are only three markets: the central market opposite St John's churchyard; the fruit and veg market in Barrack Lane and Jacob's antiques market not far from the central station.

There is also an outdoor market across the river from the Millennium stadium that sells mainly organic food on Sunday mornings.

Cardiff Central Market

Fruit and veg stall, Cardiff Central Market

Ashton's fish stall in the Central Market is legendary. It smells to high heaven but that's fish for you: smelly, as if they are getting their own back for being plucked out of their natural environment and onto a slab. It all looks so wholesome. Have you ever tried gurnard, grilse, trigger fish or dorado? And the stall sells venison, quail and quails' eggs, wild boar and pheasant – a veritable mediaeval feast. Wenches are not provided. Interesting how game can conjure up an image of rumbustious banqueting, unlike fish. A fillet of hake or baked mackerel doesn't have the same epicurean appeal. Sorry about this but Ashton's could be the 'sole' of Cardiff!

In the central market you can get your hair cut, eat

faggots, peas and chips; buy a kitten, bird or fish; find highly unusual vegetables; get your watch fixed and have your fortune told – but not at the same stall. There is also a stall dedicated to walking sticks. **Fresh and Simple** is a stall that sells a huge range of vegetables and fruit. For your next roast dinner forget about potatoes, carrots, cabbage and peas. Instead pile on the eddoes, pak choi, mooli and cho cho followed not by the traditional rice pudding but a hearty helping of Dragon Fruit – as long as you are not going to work the next morning. The proprietor – Mr Norbert Zwilling – is from Heidelberg in Germany and has been running his stall for three years.

Demand for his more unusual fare comes from Cardiff's diverse ethnic minority groups – Chinese, Afro-Caribbean, Indian, Pakistanis, Bangladeshi. Most of the goods are delivered from London and Birmingham. The local veg and fruit market in Bessemer Road does not cater for other than mainstream palates. There are Cardiffians I know who would rate broccoli and sweetcorn as frighteningly exotic – and as for kiwi fruit…

A market trader all on his own is **Max**, short for Maxim. He is the Sioni Winwns from Brittany. Two misconceptions need to be laid to rest about Max; first he is not itinerant. He and his fellow Breton traders have a house in Ninian Park Road, Cardiff. They travel throughout Wales with their garlic and onions but (second misconception) not on bikes but in a blue van. Max is a happy, talkative young man who stands near Hayes Island, not like some street traders, shouting to passers-by – but mute as if intent on hiding the fact that he speaks fluent English and possibly a very passable Welsh.

Jacob's Antiques Market escaped the destiny of other buildings skirting the designated starting point of the road to the Bay. It's near the main railway station on the St Mary Street side of the city and it houses scores of bric-a-brac and specialist mini-shops. There is another antiques market in one of the arcades but that's on the twee side and rather pricey. Jacob's is different. Most of the sellers there are sociable and prepared to negotiate.

But alas, the market is shrinking before our eyes. The old clothes shop Tails and the Unexpected – all mothballs, dinner jackets, spats and ball gowns – has moved out to Penarth, and gone, too, is the 1950s and 1960s stall along with past hits on LPs and EPs and the wonderful radio stall. Traders there will tell you that Ikea has brought a new minimalist and affordable allure to potential market customers. The old has given way to the new.

Jacob's Antiques Market

But one stall that is still going well is the **Goth Horror** collection, open at the weekends. Jimmy who owns it is from Newcastle and works the rest of the week (Monday to Thursday) in the Welsh Tartan store near the castle. Trade was given a boost when Prince Harry donned a Nazi armband for a fancy dress party. As a result, even little old ladies were buying Nazi flags from Jimmy. Much of the stock is reproduction. There are not that many SS Gestapo uniforms knocking around. As you might expect, Jimmy is in demand by TV for props. While Jimmy with his Mohican haircut, earrings, black leather outfit and boots merges almost imperceptibly into his memorabilia in Jacob's market, does he don full tartan regalia the rest of the week? You'll need to visit the Welsh Tartan centre in High Street Arcade to find the answer.

But avoid, I beg you, the caff in Jacob's Market. It does not aspire to be a greasy spoon. In fact, it hardly aspires to be anything, serving instant coffee and a range of snacks ranging from toast to Welsh cakes, with nothing in between. It oozes all the charm of a homeless person's drop-in centre. Perhaps the Welsh cakes are antiques. Try one and let me know.

The Goth Horror collection at Jacob's Antiques Market

Casinos

Quite a step from the homeliness of markets is the casino. Surely the mark of a sophisticated city is the presence of casinos – although there is probably a world of difference culturally between Monte Carlo and Las Vegas. Nevertheless, the word 'casino' still retains an aura of James Bond and wealthy people who own yachts rather than coracles.

Cardiff has a number of casinos apart from the one in the Bay, the oldest being **Les Croupiers** in St Mary Street, but the capital city is in the running after recent legislation to accommodate a huge regional casino. No doubt it will be down the Bay. The odd feature of Les Croupiers is that it spawned a running club that competes in long distance races. Indeed, the founder was a former athlete who pipped me for second place in an under-15 Welsh cross-country championship. His name, I seem to recall, is Gordon something – an unusual surname. Although I have never set foot in one of these places of pleasure – or misery – I know someone who works in one, and I am told that the big punters are Chinese. This makes sense since the recent exodus to the UK of citizens of Hong Kong after the handover to China has meant an increase in the numbers of people who – back in their own country – were disbarred from betting by law. This meant, of course, that rather like prohibition in the USA, there developed a thriving underworld of betting on horseracing and on British Premier League football results. My visits to Malaysia and Hong Kong confirmed that betting is a genetic characteristic of Chinese males.

In Wales, apart from casinos, the only other main venue

for betting is Chepstow Racecourse. Unless, of course, you include the pony-and-trap races held in remote locations in west and north Wales and which are covered on the Welsh language TV channel S4C. These races are the equestrian equivalent of watching female athletes competing in crinolines.

Cardiff clubs and societies

Surely we can discover the soul of Cardiff in the numerous clubs and societies that flourish in and around the centre. This is what Cardiff is all about.

Look in the yellow pages and you will find hundreds of clubs and societies. Most of them are social clubs – which is a euphemism for drinking places often with cheaper booze than in pubs. At the elite end is the Cardiff County Club, a second home for retired judges and people who chair quangos.

Then there is the strangely named Electricity Club near Llandaff Fields. Is this a social gathering-place for current [!] and former employees of the South Wales Electricity Board – or does it offer stimulating experiences for patrons with a particular penchant for shock treatment – perhaps administered by someone dressed up as a nurse?

Political clubs are not always what they seem. Who, for example, attends the Conservative Clubs in the Riverside and Grangetown areas of Cardiff? Without being too insulting, these are the most down-at-heel, ethnically-diverse areas of the city. Take away the Muslim citizens (who would not be too attracted to the prospect of cheap alcoholic drinks), and those unfortunates on welfare benefits, and you are not left with too many locals committed to the Tory view of the world.

In the old days, in parts of Wales which were dry on a Sunday, you joined the Labour and Conservative clubs for a drink on the Sabbath even though you might have been a devout communist.

But delve deeper beneath the surface of spurious political associations and bingo palaces and you will find clubs dedicated to activities that are above the commonplace. May I recommend the **Beermat Collectors Society**. This is a very select group of devotees of the beermat who are part of a British movement to preserve the often soggy protectors of polished tables. The Cardiff group meets in the Cayo Arms in Cathedral Road biannually – once in Spring and again in Autumn. If this seems to be a somewhat unclubbable club, there are occasions when collectors can meet with like-minded people in England. So what do members – there are about 20-30 in Cardiff – do when they meet? No prizes here. They exchange – swap – BEER MATS. But do not think for one moment that these honourable people steal them from pubs. They always ask the landlord or whoever is behind the bar and they are often given unused mats to take away.

Since the Brains Brewery has a virtual monopoly in Cardiff, one could perhaps be rather sceptical of the variety of beer mats that are swapped during the course of a meeting in the Cayo Arms.

So please – if there is a would-be brewer out there who could introduce a note of competition (Tomos Watkin tried and were then taken over – but the beer is still around) – please come to Cardiff and give us an alternative to the uninspired offerings of Brains. It is an insult to the Welsh beer-swilling public that the strongest beer Brains produces – Brains SA, sometimes known as 'skull attack' – is a wimpish 4.2% ABV. The English beat us hands down. Fullers, Youngs, Adnams – to name but three – produce real ales in the upper 5% and over 6% strengths. Skull attack? Do me a favour. The local micro-brewery Bullmastiff is beginning to make itself known, but it needs to live up to its name in its marketing.

The existence of other brewers would also make the

meetings of the Cardiff section of the beermat collectors' society far more exciting than they already are. STOP PRESS: the Vale of Glamorgan brewery has just started up. Good luck.

Perhaps there could be a merger between the Beermat Collectors' Society and the Cardiff-based **South Wales Postcard Club.** Old postcards could be laminated so that they could be used as beer mats. This would multiply the number of different beer mats that would be on offer for swapping or selling to fellow enthusiasts and increase the club's membership tenfold, or even more.

A thought arises: can beer mats be legitimately used to absorb the spillage from wine glasses or whisky tumblers? Or are they designed exclusively for beer glasses? Not even Brains beer mats should have to suffer the indignity of being placed under glasses filled with lager. People over the age of forty who order lager in pubs serving real ale should be evicted unceremoniously as untutored blackguards.

Let us forego the dubious pleasures of a cheap drink at the 4th Glamorgan Home Guard Club located in Ely and instead enquire about membership of the Ladies Barbershop Harmony Club in Fairwater or the South East Wales Beaders Society to be found in Llandaff. Ladies, what are you waiting for?

Of course, if you are a particularly tall lady, you could do worse than apply to join the **Tall Persons Club** run by a gentleman in Llanishen. He is 7ft 2ins or whatever that is in metres, and is featured on the UK Tall Persons website. The tallest person in Britain is 7ft 6ins. (To be admitted to the club you need to be at least 6ft tall if you are a woman and 6ft 5ins for a man. In the Cardiff club – since we Celts tend to be smaller – a female must be 5ft 10ins or more, and a man

6ft 2ins.) Most of the social events are held outside Cardiff but the Wales group gets together occasionally on a Friday night. The group is there to provide support for younger tall people who are often taunted at school and there are also legal issues to deal with from time to time such as adapting working environments to suit people who can't get their legs under desks. Interestingly, there does not appear to be a short persons' club around.

When I discovered that there was a **Hedgehog Helpline** service working in the Whitchurch area I had a vision of a small prickly creature equipped with a dinky mobile phone.

"Hello. My name's Harry. Yes, Harry Hedgehog.

"Which service do you require?"

"I'd like the 'Get you Home Unsquashed' service."

"Right, could you give me your location?"

"I'm near the A470 by Pontypridd. I need to get back to Cardiff without crossing any roads."

"You're a long way from Cardiff. What happened?"

"I was following a scent to a female hedgehog and…"

"Yes, I understand. We'll send the Hedgehog Heli. It should spot you from up there with its Hedgehog Heatray spotlight."

But no – the Hedgehog Helpline is all about rescuing orphaned prickly creatures and has been in operation for nearly eighteen years. In the Cardiff area between 300–500 hedgehogs are rescued each year. How, you might ask, do you recognise an orphaned from a family-intact hedgehog? Easy. Orphaned hedgehogs emit a squeaking sound as they wander about. A team of volunteers gather in the orphans and do their best to rehabilitate them back into the community. Just as there is no short persons club in Cardiff, there is no helpline for abandoned badgers, bunnies or moles. A similar charity, however, does exist for cats.

Catwel has its 'headquarters' in Cyncoed but the volunteers work not only with privileged cats. The network covers the whole of Cardiff and seeks to keep down the population of feral cats and find homes for cats that are social outcasts. My family were once about to put a very scabby cat out of its misery and arranged to take it to the vet to have it put down, only to find out in the nick of time that it belonged to the bloke next door.

We also took in an abandoned cat as one of the family, and having accepted it as one of us, we had it neutered. We never saw it again. A friend of mine said that had he been the cat, he'd have had second thoughts about staying around too.

One group exclusively for women is the **Morris Side** – why 'side' is a mystery and 'Morris' is probably a corruption of 'Moorish'. This dance group was started in 1973 by the merger of a Folk Club and Mountaineering Club. Did they meet in Clwb Ifor Bach in Cardiff or on the top of Snowdon? The ladies dance to the tunes of two musicians – one playing a melodeon and the other a whistle, a type of recorder. Exactly why they banned men is not known. Possibly they thought they looked somewhat camp trotting here and there waving hankies and dressed like rejects from a Tyrolean oompah band.

Morris dancing is, of course, a traditional English village pastime along with cricket, hunting and being rude to strangers. However, these terpsichorean adepts (dancers) also include Welsh dances in their repertoire. It is difficult to imagine an all-male Morris group (side) being started in Cardiff, although it might catch on in certain establishments in Charles Street. More on this later.

So – there you have it – tall persons, hedgehogs, postcards, beer mats, bust-to-bust dancing. We are spoilt for choice in Cardiff.

It is, of course, a sad fact that there is no club in Cardiff dedicated to the pursuit of excellence among the myriad lavatories dotted around the city centre. There are numerous guides to other bodily functions such as eating and drinking so why not a guide to toileting?

Toilets

Had I sub-contracted part of this section to a female, I would have been able to provide a 100% guide to all the best watering holes in and around the city.

How many tardis toilets are still dotted around? The one in Albany Road was one I tried but claustrophobia set in once the doors closed, and I was fearful about being locked in there for several days. They are probably sound-proofed as well.

The most famous toilets in Cardiff must be the ones on **Hayes Island**, opposite Habitat. This little haven of continental squalor has subterranean toilets set beneath the eating space. The combination of essence of urine wafting up as you gnash into a sausage bap is probably unique in the annals (careful) of alfresco cuisine. Still, the pigeons do well out of it. But beware, there are three entrances but only two sexes so there is an opportunity to run down the wrong set of steps and end up in unfamiliar surroundings – in my case a sudden lack of urinals. I have it on excellent authority that the ladies' facilities are salubrious. Indeed, at Christmas there is festive piped music and decorations. To men 'going to the toilet' is a solitary occasion even though we might be standing shoulder to shoulder. To women, who usually go in pairs when they are in a pub, it could be a ploy to get away from the men and have a chat.

Who on earth would choose to work in such places? Probably the same sort of person who is happy to make dead people look lovely in their coffins, and pathologists. Other people's bodily functions are not my cup of tea – a very strange tea-bag that would be.

The entrance to the subterranean Hayes Island toilets

Nearby, there are more public toilets opposite Debenhams, just alongside the open veg and fruit market – a planner's paradise. They have good access for disabled customers, which is not the case on Hayes Island. There are other and rather more sanitary public toilets in the newish shopping malls – the Capitol and Queens: not – to use a well-worn pun – lavish – but acceptable. Praise be to the Millennium Arts Centre. It has the only fragrant male toilets in Cardiff.

You would expect the very best in Howells – the posh department store. But certainly the gents' facilities are nothing to write home about; not an armchair in sight, and distinctly lacking in space. If I'm spending real money on quality goods, I expect the best in the toilet division: that means state-of-the-art technology: soap, water and a hot drier that performs when you put your hands under a stainless steel console.

Hayes Island is not just a centre for eating and toileting. It attracts craft sellers, pigeons and street musicians.

Street musicians

Do not confuse the street musicians of Cardiff with buskers. The word 'to busk' is assumed to be a nautical term meaning to cruise about. So buskers are people who move around. In Cardiff, the performers have their designated spots: the crooner in Queen Street, the Samba band in the Hayes, the guitarist outside Waterstones. The exception is the street philosopher and drummer who spends time in the Atlantic coffee house, but is prepared to offer his thoughts on life to any audience he chooses. He calls himself **Ninjah Pendragon**. A tall, impressive man, often wearing a military tunic but sometimes draped in a Welsh flag, Ninjah (his spelling) was born in Lewisham of Jamaican parents. He has break-danced in America. He was educated in Birmingham, later came to Wales to 'find some roots', and has recently brought out a CD. He loves Cardiff and says that if London is the city of gold, Cardiff is platinum. He drums on Council street furniture (litter bins) because his mission in life is to give people good vibrations. "I free people from constipation and people are going to the toilet all around me." He sees

Ninjah Pendragon

greed as the worst enemy and loves Wales because it still holds to family values. The city, he says, is full of characters. It's got soul and spirit and the women are the most beautiful in the world. There should be more outlets for arts and crafts and the clubs need to stay open later.

In winter he becomes the sunshine and he keeps the people warm.

Samba Galêz is a community percussion group formed in 1990. They hold workshops on Saturday mornings in Willows School in the Tremorfa area and the music is based on 'afro-centric rhythms' which have become the traditional fare of the renowned carnival in Brazil. The band has not played there

Samba Galêz

yet but has performed at Glastonbury, the Brecon Jazz Festival and at the Samba Encounter in Brighton.

The band's leader, Simon Preston, has been a musician and composer for 25 years, travelling to such places as Brazil, Cuba, Tanzania, and the USA to learn his craft. The roots of the band's music lie in Brazilian, Cuban, and African rhythms. Catch the band on most Saturday afternoons performing in Hayes Island.

What is the attraction of playing in the band? One of its longer-serving players is Kim from Penarth. She joined after hearing the band playing in their usual spot in the Hayes on a Saturday afternoon. She says it's a technical challenge playing different rhythms and the band is like a family. They even go away for social weekends together. They play in many parts of the UK and have performed in Ireland but the best gigs are still those in the Hayes.

> "What – just drumming and banging and shaking? No music?"
>
> "Depends what you mean by 'music'."
>
> "Well, tunes, melodies, singing."
>
> "This lot are versatile. They do gigs with some of them playing the violin and accordion and sometimes, such as on their CDs, they break out into song. So there!"

The South Wales Intercultural Arts (**SWICA**) initiated the Samba Band through its livewire organiser Steve Fletcher, a son of Aberystwyth. Funded mainly through the Arts Council of Wales, Cardiff Council and the Heritage Lottery Fund, SWICA's main claim to fame is in developing the former Butetown Carnival into what is now known as the MAS Carnival – a vibrant parade of bands and dancers representing

Samba Galêz

the many cultural faces of Cardiff – Caribbean steel bands, a
Sikh music group, Afro-Caribbean dancers. The emphasis has
always been on youth, but at least one middle-aged local walks
demurely in drag amongst the other performers every year.

He might also be there in the annual **Mardi Gras,** now in its seventh year in Cardiff. This gay festival is held in September, and the Fringe Festival which precedes the Mardi Gras covers various venues in Cardiff. It's serious, it's outrageous – but mainly it actually epitomises the word 'gay' because it is a celebration of diversity.

The serious side is its association with the organisation 'Safer Cardiff'. One of the key aims of this body is to combat hate-crime against minority groups and the Mardi Gras event is supported financially by a range of sponsors, including the local council.

The official guide to the fest lists a number of gay pubs and clubs in the centre of Cardiff and 'queer-friendly' B&Bs. There are pubs clustered around Caroline Street – The **Golden Cross** and **Kings Cross** – which apparently are designated as comfortable venues for gays. Charles Street is also becoming a hot spot for homosexuals – sorry, but I would like to reclaim the word 'gay' for other purposes – with the **Exit Bar** (much more tasteful, I would think, than the Entrance Bar) and **Club X** (don't ask).

Whatever your sexual predilection, do join in the spirit of tolerance and diversity. But if you do, be a little more aware than I was when I wandered into a gay pub in Manchester. On my own, after a few drinks, I entered the karaoke session and afterwards was greeted with a gentle ripple of polite hand-clapping from what I later realised was an assemblage of about 35 gay men and four or five lesbians. The song I had chosen

Opposite and over the page: Outrageous costumes at the gay Cardiff Mardi Gras

to sing was 'She' an old Charles Aznavour and, more recently, Elvis Costello song. I'm surprised I wasn't ejected for being culpably offensive.

Of course, many of those attending the Mardi Gras look outrageous. What do they look like on other days of the year? We can imagine the rather fusty office manager transformed at the gay festival into a buxom tart wearing a basque and fishnet stockings.

"Hello big boy – my name is Chardonnay."
"No it's not. You're Kevin and you work in the Halifax."

There are tents and stalls galore at the outdoor event: some offer free wine and titbits, others promote the rights of gays, and there's one where your relationship can be 'blessed'. For this, couples dress up as bride and groom. I'm not sure what the customary preparations are for this type of ceremony but I would have thought that a bridal five o'clock shadow indicates a certain indifference to getting completely into the role. Nevertheless, civil partnerships are now all the rage. One woman abroad married a dolphin – a male dolphin. Nothing unusual about her.

I resisted the invitation to respond to the very tall gentleman with KISS and ME imprinted on respectively the left and right buttock, on the grounds that in polite society one should never kiss a buttock to which one has not been introduced. It's probably to do with my bourgeois upbringing.

Trevor Rees from the Rhondda Valley sings into a toy-like microphone at his pitch in Queen Street. Some call him Toymike Trevor. He prefers singing to talking. He is a full-time crooner who once busked up and down the Edgware Road and at Marble Arch in London. He has been performing in Cardiff for six years and likes it here because it's a big enough city and the people are freer with their money. At first he sang not for money but for the sheer enjoyment – and it shows.

Full-time crooner Trevor Rees

Cor Cochion – the Cardiff Reds Choir – a group formed in 1983, sings unaccompanied – usually outside the Central Market. This mixed choir – mixed vocally and politically (although the term 'red' hints at their political leanings) – has raised money for various causes. Their 'political music' attacks what they regard as social injustices across the globe. There is no cause too insignificant to espouse and bring to the public's attention, from fair wages for Venezuelan hop-pickers to free-the-political-prisoners in Llandudno. No matter that their efforts have no chance of influencing any government anywhere on the globe. They feel good about what they do and the harmony is excellent.

Mark plays his acoustic guitar all over south Wales and in Cardiff every Saturday, outside Waterstones in the Hayes.

He does this full-time and also plays in a couple of bands around Cardiff – mainly country-and-western style. He'd go down well in the valleys. Mark is from Ely in Cardiff. He doesn't sing when he plays because most of his tunes are not the type of music that needs belting out. It's quiet stuff. Mark – like all the other street musicians featured here – is very happy with life. Making music is obviously good for the soul, for the music maker and for Cardiff.

Street musician Mark

It's stretching it a bit to classify **Mr Crier, the Town Crier** as a street musician. But he regularly augments his stentorian voice by playing a hunting horn to attract attention to his vociferous announcements. Mr Crier's real name is Graham Vedmore and he lives in Caerffili. He first started 'performing' as a town crier in 1991 when he was appointed

Mr Crier, the Town Crier

town crier for Bridgend. Three years later he turned professional. In 1999 he developed the new technique of 'focussed personality projection' which sounds like a posh term for 'raving extrovert behaviour'.

Mr Crier has many other talents and at the drop of a couple of hundred quid, can transform himself into a pirate captain (boat optional), Bosun Bill (a Napoleonic sailor), a Victorian Santa Claus (as opposed, presumably, to a post-modern Santa), a wizard, a pie man, Cupid (bow and arrow not optional) and – wait for it – St Peter. Cupid is likely to be a quasi-Victorian equivalent of a stripogram but at which function St Peter would be an appropriate guest is uncertain – a wake, perhaps, or at the Jehovah's Witnesses convention sometimes held in Cardiff?

The Town Crier is a character, but an assumed and carefully constructed one. What about the 'natural' characters of Cardiff? Are they dead or hidden away in hostels? We might speculate what has become of them. There was the short man – often sporting a raincoat over his left arm – who, with a poking finger breaking the air – would remonstrate with complete strangers about some imagined wrong he had suffered. If he'd been two feet (whatever metres) taller he'd have been frightening. And whither the trolley man pushing around a collection of strange objects and followed by a gaggle or pack of dogs? Most challenging was the lady of indeterminate age who would sing and shout and, as a finale, lift up her skirt above waist-height to display everything. Not a knicker in sight. She used to attract far more attention than the town crier.

I'd wager that the finger pointing little man, abusive and opinionated as he seemed, is now a councillor; the tramp with the trolley and dogs runs Hypervalue and the woman-with-obviously-no-underwear is a reformed model working for Ann Summers. Talking of Ann Summers…

Specialist shops

Have you ever felt the urge to browse for half an hour or so among thousands of buttons? Neither have I, but one day, after a night on the town, you could wake up with a yen to do something even more outrageous than taking home a road cone. If you want buttons, **Clare Grove's** in the Castle Arcade is the place for you. If you feel adventurous enough to go into the shop, try asking this question: do you sell buttons that are guaranteed not to pop off the front of men's shirts? OR where can I buy a shirt with a zip-up front?

For grown men still interested in playing with trains, wonderland awaits. The **Ian Allan** bookshop and models store in the Royal Arcade sells hundreds of books and life-like models of trains and planes and very little else. A glance at the shelves in W H Smith reveals an obvious market for such commodities and periodicals of consuming interest to those whose idea of a thrilling afternoon's pleasure is manoeuvring small radio-controlled boats on the waters of Roath Park. *Diecast Collector, Doll's House Magazine* and *Model Rail* make some anoraks salivate more than any 'top shelf' magazines would.

Mention needs to be made of what is reputedly the oldest record shop in the world. **Spillers** in the Hayes opened in 1894 in the Queens Arcade. It originally specialised in phonographs, shellac discs and sheet music. Despite the slicker attractions of Virgin and HMV, Spillers is thriving. It's tiny but always packed – the opposite of St David's Hall on a has-beens night.

There are shops selling German tankards and Welsh kilts, and there's **Wally's** in the Royal Arcade – the very first delicatessen in Cardiff, which sells the best home-made humus in town. At a time when chicken in the basket was considered to be the height of culinary sophistication, Wally's began tempting the Cardiff palate with olive oil, strange-looking sausages, pasta and snails. Now, despite the exotic continental delicacies filling the shelves of most supermarkets, Wally's remains the only shop dedicated entirely to the sale of food that most Cardiffians only saw on holiday. The Chinese food stores in Riverside and halal meat providers in the same area and in Grangetown are niche markets for locals and for many people outside Cardiff whose culinary efforts amount to more than the customary Brit-Welsh cuisine.

It is doubtful, though, whether you will find in Cardiff's oriental food stores any of the more out-of-the-way delicacies eaten by the Chinese in their own countries. The day that your average Chinese take-away starts offering jellyfish, snake soup or chicken claws on the menu is when you'll know real Chinese food is taking hold.

If you want to keep rather than eat more unusual creatures or parts of them, you can take home a friendly stick insect or python; perhaps a lizard or two or a house-trained armadillo. They are all in **Dragon Reptiles** on Cowbridge Road East in Canton. And should you be unfortunate enough to get bitten by one of these creatures, you could probably find a cure in one of the alternative medicine shops in Cardiff, notably the Chinese medicine outlet on Queen Street and in the St David's Centre. There in mysterious containers are oriental treatments for any ailment you can think of – from

flat feet to flatulence; boils, bunions, baldness, backache
– there will be an alleged cure. Be bold. Try essence of frog's
testicles or root of mandrake; lie down and have little needles
stuck into your skin. Even if there's nothing wrong with
you, it's worth it if only to introduce a slightly different
conversation-piece over dinner with friends.

In Cardiff there are aromatherapists, hypnotherapists,
reflexologists, chiropractors, herbalists, homeopaths, and
osteopaths and if none of these treatments works, take a bus
ride to Caerphilly Road, and at the southern end of Pantbach
Road you will find a shop selling crystals and stones, all in the
name of complementary therapies.

Quite recently, interest has been growing in alternative
Welsh attire. No longer the pointed hats invented by
the gracious and eccentric Lady Llanover and worn by
schoolchildren on St David's Day. Gone too are the Dai caps
and clogs, worn now only at eisteddfodau when young men
jump over a broomstick as they perform a traditional dance.
Today, a shop in the Castle Arcade sells kilts ('cilts' is the
Welsh version). Call me a sceptic, but I'm not aware of any
McThomasses, McLloyds or McEvanses in any telephone
directories in Cardiff or in any other parts of Wales. But, the
Wales Tartan shop tells us in their leaflet that the Welsh wore
fashion 'akin to kilts two thousand years ago, probably with
a form of leather trousers or leggings wrapped around with
rope'. How do they know, you might ask. No wall paintings of
men in cilts have been found but, the same leaflet informs us,
a ninth century stone carving has been found depicting a man
wearing a cilt. It does not say where or by whom.

To hire a full cilt outfit for one night will cost you twice
as much as many people pay to buy a suit. Still, you are likely

to cut a dash, as they say, as you do your late night shopping at Asda.

Trying to squeeze a Welshman into a kilt can be taken as a metaphor for the kind of cultural and ethnic assimilation that people are proud of in Cardiff. Perhaps the essence or soul of Cardiff is its very own blend of Welsh and other cultures – its amalgam of diversity. Where better to discover a tinge of continental character than the inviting shop in Castle Arcade called **Madame Fromage**. In distance, this is a pasty's throw away from the Central Market, but in the goodies it sells it is several hundred miles away and even more kilometres. For here you will find a veritable cornucopia of Gallic cheeses, wines, terrines, oils and other delicacies. Mainly, though, you will find cheeses; cheeses with names fit for a banquet at Versailles.

Here in Cardiff the French cheeses sound decidedly cheesy. Not many Cardiffians would have the gall (Gaul?) to walk in and ask for a bit of Reblochon de Savoie or a soupcon of Chevre de Sainte-Maure de Touraine. Better, perhaps, to ask for a quarter kilo of Stinking Bishop than to try to get one's tongue round Vacherin l'ecorce de Sapin. But thankfully not all the fromages are galloise. There is an impressive list of Welsh cheeses including the much-loved Nantybwla and Llanboidy offerings. I look forward to the day when, in a Parisian restaurant, I shall be able to order a Chablis with my 'fromage de Nantybwla s'il vous plait'.

Mysteries of Cardiff

So far, we have been focused on the familiar and recognisable in Cardiff. But what about the unknown corners of the capital city? There are no infamous ghosts inhabiting any well-known buildings in Cardiff. You might have expected some apparition walking the ramparts of the castle or the ethereal chanting coming from the site of the friary in Greyfriars Road. Yet let's dig beneath the stereotypes. There are deeper unexplained phenomena as we seek the soul of this capital city. For example, why is the fortune teller's stall in Cardiff Market never open? Has Mr Petulengro foreseen a dread happening that prevents him making the trip from home to the city centre? There is an alternative clairvoyant – a lady ready to read your palm in St Mellons, to the east of the city centre. She can probably tell you when the Number 5 bus is likely to turn up (to the nearest day).

Here's another mystery. Is the only beekeeper listed in the area phone book really called Mr Wasp? And where have all the waterways in Cardiff gone? Within living memory, water flowed down Churchill Way, down the bustling Mill Lane area and under the bridge near the Central Hotel at the southern end of St Mary Street. At one time Cardiff was a Welsh Venice. The Glamorganshire canal carried boats bringing iron, tin and coal to the thriving docks. The feeder is still visible skirting the New Theatre, and the Taff once coursed along Westgate Street. Along its stretch was a main boarding point at what is now Quay Street.

Where has all this water gone? Under concrete or tarmac as roads were built to serve the new commercialism of retail as the docks withered? That doesn't explain the disappearance of the moat fronting the castle that is now just grass.

There are other, even more prosaic mysteries about Cardiff. For example, were Cardiff Arms Park, Brains Dark and Clark's pies named in order for the Cardiff accent to be displayed in all its melodious glory? These items, in the Cardiff dialect, come out as Cairdiff Airms Pairk, Brains Dairk and Clairks pie with 'pie' sounding half way between 'pi' and 'poi'. What, too, of the Welsh delicacy – chicken curry off the bone airff 'n airff? The true Cardiffian has an accent in the same mellifluous bracket as Scouse, Geordie and Brummy but not quite as attractive as the sound of the Llanelli or north Walian vocal sound. Perhaps we have discovered the soul of Cardiff. Is it to be found in the **Cardiff Accent**. Years ago we could have featured among the clubs and societies of the capital city the Cardiff Language Society, entry to which could only be gained by articulating 'airff a dairk un a Mairmite sairnie' in the received Standard Cardiff accent. Members used to meet in a club on Newport Road and one of them used to play the accordion in a posh French restaurant opposite the New Theatre. But he would never speak in case he gave the game away as he was known professionally as Pierre.

Perhaps, then, the soul of Cardiff lies in its distinctive accent. This is what distinguishes us from even our nearest neighbour, Newport which has a watered down version of true Cardiffian. There is no greater experience (this could, on reflection, be a slight overstatement) than hearing the true Cardiff accent flowing from the mouths of black, Asian and middle eastern citizens of our capital city. One day we might also hear the same sound on the lips of the oriental among us. What a prospect! A 'multi-coloured airmony' of sound. Granted, some of us might have broader tastes than a Clairgeys poi or arf u Dairk but chicken tikka masairla and a pint u sairky sound just as good.

Another mystery unique to Cardiff is how all those different animals got stuck trying to jump over the castle wall and then turned to stone.

Sport

One of the mysteries in the sporting context is how a Welshman can play a sport for England. If you are Welsh you have to play cricket for England if you want to play at the highest level. In rugby, you need only to have lived in Wales for three years before qualifying to play for Wales and, of course, vice versa for those (turncoats) who are Welsh but who decided to play for England. Probably none of the Wales soccer team could sing the national anthem – which is a bit of a mystery in itself.

Some of the performances of Welsh teams remain a mystery. The **Cardiff Rugby Union** team are not called the Blues for nothing. For a number of seasons that is the mental state in which they have left their supporters. In order to attract more people through the turnstiles, Cardiff – like other sides – have introduced some elements of razz-a-ma-tazz. After a score for the home team, children bang on the hoardings and a furious blast of something almost resembling music bursts through the air. This is the main reason why many grown adults stay away from home games. Strangely enough, they would prefer to watch a winning team well away from this sordid attempt to cater for a very small number of under-12s.

Cardiff City Football Club – the Bluebirds – have also subjected their fans to a roller-coaster emotional ride over the past few seasons – latterly just avoiding relegation. Cardiff – of course – remain the only club to have taken the FA Cup out of England after they beat Arsenal 1–0 in 1927. Since the Scottish clubs have their own cup tournament and the only other Welsh clubs in the Football League are Swansea and Wrexham, this achievement takes on less of a momentous significance.

Some of the club's more moronic followers have gained notoriety as the Soul Crew. They inhabit a world of football terrorism in which the sole rationale for goading or physically attacking supporters of other clubs is that they are supporters of other clubs. Why don't they get a life and take up fishing or croquet?

The **Cardiff Devils** ice hockey team too has been in a yoyo situation over the years. Their rink is due to be transplanted to somewhere in the Bay. Ice Hockey is fast fun, and even cricket has latched on to the modern emphasis on speed and noise. Glamorgan play at Sophia Gardens and have done well in limited overs competitions. But they too have sunk back into something less than mediocrity. Is there something about the Welsh sporting psyche that says: 'OK, we've done well now, *chwarae teg*, let someone else have a go'. After the recent Grand Slam and the results that followed, I'm beginning to believe it.

The **Cardiff International Arena** holds professional boxing bouts and wrestling promotions. The boxing is real but the wrestling is a well-orchestrated pantomime created and performed for spectators with an aggregate IQ of 3. Recently, the **Wales Rally GB** – part of the World Rally Championship, has had its finishing line at the Millennium Stadium after several riotous days in the forests of Powys. **Cycling** as a spectator sport has never been popular in Wales but the terrain surely lends itself to the rigours of a world championship competition. Wales has, of course, its own cycling heroine – Nicole Cooke.

In and around the city you can watch baseball, hockey, and kids performing impressively on skateboards. But alas, no more speedway – except on special occasions at the Millennium Stadium – no more roller skating (formerly catered for in a special centre in Cathays) or betting on the dogs (at the old Arms Park) or on the horses (in Ely).

In fact, many Cardiffians would be unaware of the many sporting venues now disappeared under concrete. There was a stadium in Grangetown which hosted many fine athletics tournaments; the speedway and greyhound racing stadium in Sloper Road near the Cardiff City Football ground. Later, the speedway venue changed to a site in nearby Penarth Road but crowds diminished until the track closed in 1953.

Where the Cardiff Royal Infirmary now stands was the Cardiff Bicycle Ground where, in 1897, David Stanton, the English penny farthing cycling champion, set a world record for fifty miles before a capacity crowd. In Westgate Street, now a wide thoroughfare hosting one of the main entrances to the Millennium Stadium, there was a skating rink where one of Cardiff's most renowned sporting heroes – Jim Driscoll – won and lost various bouts. Other boxing venues now gone were in Dumfries Place and Greyfriars Road, the latter location having yielded its priceless derelict monastic treasure to more mundane fleshpots only four or five decades ago.

But let's celebrate the outstanding achievements of two Cardiff legends – Tanni Grey-Thompson and Colin Jackson in the sphere of athletics. Joe Calzaghe, a world-champion – often boxes in Cardiff. These are people who have kicked the trend of Welsh sporting fly-by-nights and remained at the top of their profession for many years as, of course, many have in the performing arts.

The Arts

Of course, like most large cities, Cardiff caters for mainstream culture. For theatre there is the **New Theatre** in Park Place/Greyfriars Road and the **Sherman** in Senghenydd Road; for ballet and opera the **Millennium Centre** is the main venue; the **National Museum** houses a huge range of paintings and sculpture, stuffed animals (not the museum guides), pottery and relics of a more primitive civilisation (no, not the museum guides). The actual museum guides have been specially trained to sleep standing up but will spring back to consciousness when asked intelligent, searching questions such as 'Where are the toilets?' or 'Can I leave the baby with you for an hour or so?' and there are a number of multiplex cinemas dotted round the city centre. **St David's Hall** stages anything from stand-up comedians to tribute bands and often rather sad, aged has-beens whose last hit was 45 years ago and who play to an audience of three. The **Cardiff International Arena** – deliberately seeking the abbreviated version CIA – it could have been CICentre – is more inclined towards current icons of popular music including rap artists who manage to sneer their way tunelessly through interminable episodes of contrived and vacuous rhymes.

For the more esoterically-minded devotees of culture, **Chapter Arts Centre** in the Canton area offers terribly intense and meaningful films with sub-titles; experimental presentations from porn to poetry; exhibitions of art created by aspiring latter-day hippies and off-the-wall showcases such as dancing to the absence of music.

Other venues for new 'talent' to expose itself is the **Gate** – a converted (sorry) church in Keppoch Street off City Road and the **Toucan Club** in Newport Road. Diversions is a well-established dance group in Cardiff, and there are several small art galleries that exhibit and sell the work of local artists.

All the suburban cinemas have now gone, the last being the Monico in Rhiwbina which managed to sustain a two-cinema facility against all the odds, but was also criminally guilty of hiding a superb 1930's exterior under the façade of what can most accurately be described as a corrugated air-raid shelter.

Café Jazz on St Mary Street is almost the sole purveyor of jazz in Cardiff unless you count the rather sombre jazz scene at the Riverside, or at the Inn on the River, now to be converted into flats (nb: 'flats' in Riverside; 'Apartments' down the Bay). Now, on Thursdays, you can hear jazz in the Conway pub in Pontcanna.

But for the more musically discerning, you can hire the services of Aubrey – the Great Ginger Growler; the Absolute Bliss Wedding Duo or Donato Niro (aka Dai the Voice?), Italian tenor – all local acts ready to make your function memorable – one way or another.

But the pinnacle of Cardiff's achievement as a centre for the arts is the biennial **Cardiff Singer of the World** competition held at St David's Hall. It's difficult to believe that when Bryn Terfel competed he only won the lieder section, not the main competition. I met Bryn once and told him that I, too was a baritone. He did not feel threatened.

One venue that has been metamorphosed over the years is **The Point** in the old part of the Docks. This centre for a variety of musical performances was a former chapel which, in the more sordid dirty-mackintosh days of the 1960s and 70s became a strip club. Over the arch which led to the artistes' changing rooms was inscribed: 'Abandon hope all ye that enter here'. Hope of what was not made clear, but I think it refers to the reason why I don't frequent clubs of that sort.

Still on the religious theme, the **Norwegian Church** now in the Bay provides a homely atmosphere for music and art. It is the venue for performances in the Early Music programme of concerts but only seats about 40 with occasional use of a balcony upstairs to augment the audience. The problem with such a small area is that you are exposed. There is no hiding place. If, as some of us once were, you are desperately struggling to muffle your laughter as you sit in the front row listening to the pigeon-like cooing of a counter tenor, you tend to be visible – especially to the man with the high voice.

The former church is open for teas seven days a week and offers very pleasing views of the waterside. It was built in 1868 between the East and West Docks and was moved to its present location in 1987. The writer, Roald Dahl was baptised there and he lived much of his life in the leafy suburb of Radyr. The church is situated on what is claimed as the longest city waterfront in Europe.

But to end at the beginning…

10

Cardiff Soul 2

After all this, what is the essence of Cardiff? What or where is its 'soul'? Everyone who lives here would probably have a different answer. For me, the soul of a city does not lie in its buildings, although they tell a story about what a city once was, and what it still is, to a large extent. Neither – and this to many is heresy I imagine – do we need to have an in-depth knowledge of the past to appreciate the place where we have lived and grown up. Cardiff was once one of the busiest ports in the world, and with that came all the bustle and character that once was the docks area. Along with Marseilles, Cardiff was the main centre of the white slave trade right up to the 1920s. That's character for you – but do we regret its passing?

Cardiff is compact. Because it is bounded by the sea it can only spread in three directions – and to the east and the west, Newport and Penarth would not want to become city suburbs. To the north, the valleys really start only six miles away – at Tongwynlais, Taffs Well and Nantgarw.

Because the idea of a 'soul' carries with it the notion of uniqueness, the essential quality of a city has to be its originality. Take away the litany of cloned retail outlets across Britain which are on the high street and in the out-of-town malls of every town and city in the UK and what is left? Lots of places in Wales and elsewhere have castles, concert halls, and theatres. They all have pubs, bars and restaurants, churches and chapels. They might not have the cumbersome singularity of a Millennium Centre or the presence in the heart of the city of a huge sports stadium, but two mammoth buildings cannot encapsulate the character of Cardiff.

What makes the city unique are its characters: the street musicians, some of them a little eccentric; the odd societies, market stalls and specialist shops; the definitive Cardiff accent. The soul of Cardiff resides to an extent in its larger-than-life people – ordinary yet extraordinary people. After travelling away and abroad, what delights and comforts me when I come back is not so much the familiar landmarks, but the 'Cardiff-ness' of the people. The idea of a place having a spirit or soul goes back thousands of years. But there is nothing mystical about Cardiff. The endearing nature of the unusual only serves to make the commonplace more lovable.